All about Angels

A Biblical Look at God's Messengers

JILL HARTMAN

CPH
SAINT LOUIS

Editor: Thomas A. Nummela
Illustrated by Thom Buttner

Your comments and suggestions concerning the material are appreciated. Please write the Product Manager, Youth and Adult Bible Studies, Concordia Publishing House, 3558 S. Jefferson Avenue, St. Louis, MO 63118-3968.

2   3   4   5   6   7   8   9   10   07   06   05   04   03   02   01   00   99   98

contents

About the Author

Jill Hartman is a professional director of Christian education, wife, mother, and writer. For the past several years, Jill has been requested to do dozens of presentations to groups of adults and teens about angels, a topic to which she has devoted considerable time and study.

She is frequently asked whether her presentation material is available in a form that would allow groups and individuals to explore what the Bible says about angels—well, now it is!

Thanks, Jill, for sharing your work with others.

Introduction

This book comes about due to the tremendous popularity of angels these days (discussed in session 1 in this book). The wide variety, and quality, of angel information and images suggest that Christians take a careful look at what the Bible says about these amazing messengers from God.

These four study sessions will help young people and adults do just that. They look in detail at the biblical record under four headings: (1) Angels—Fad or Fact? (2) What Are Angels Like? (3) What Do Angels Do? and (4) Angels—Evil and Good. The studies are designed for sessions of about one hour in length. For every session, options are provided that could extend the study or replace other content in the study. In every case the leader is encouraged to examine the study carefully well before class time in order to choose the best activities, adapt them to his or her unique needs and setting, and evaluate the estimated schedule. Such preparation will pay big dividends.

This Bible study is uniquely suited for use with intergenerational groups of youth and adults. The topic will appeal to them equally and the study material is easily accessible to the wide range of ages such a group entails, whether it is a group of teenagers and their parents or a mixed group of youth and adults. In many cases optional instructions are provided in the teaching material to adapt this material for a mixed age group. In addition, the final section of this introduction provides some basic principles to keep in mind when working with such a group.

Careful Observation of the Biblical Record

There is no lack of evidence from the Bible for the existence of God's angels, their appearance, and the purposes for which God uses them. There are more than 250 references to angels or angelic creatures of God in Scripture.

The majority of these Bible passages are short—two or three verses. This has made it necessary to include more Bible passages in each lesson for the participant's study than is ideal. It is also true that the context for these short passages is frequently of great importance. We have therefore resisted the temptation to print out the biblical material on the resource pages, preferring that the Bible student have the Bible itself open for reading and study. (A Bible study leader with one of the many popular Bible text software programs could, of course, make study pages for each class. This might be especially valuable for participants who may be unfamiliar with the locations of the Bible books.)

As we read and study about these creatures of God, the context of Scripture reveals at least four major kinds of references.

The first category of Bible references is *actual encounters* with angels on earth. The rescue of Lot and his family (Genesis 19); the interpreting angel in Zechariah; the angels who announce the births of John and Jesus (Luke 1–2) and the resurrection (Matthew 28 and John 20); and the angel who rescues Peter from prison (Acts 12) are all examples. Each of these angel encounters gives helpful information about these unique creatures of God; they provide direct testimony about the appearance and activity of angels.

The second category consists of *visions and dreams* in which people encounter angels and angelic creatures. These visions usually portray the heavenly service of angels before the throne of God. Jacob's dream of angels descending from and ascending to heaven (Genesis 28:12); Ezekiel's vision of the four "living creatures" (Ezekiel 1); Zechariah's visions, the seraphs of Isaiah's vision (Isaiah 6); and the many angels in John's vision on the island of Patmos (Revelation 1 and nearly every chapter from 5 to the end) are all examples. Because these are visions, the language may not be literal. The events and activities pictured may have symbolic meaning. While these sections of God's Word are true and impart God's true message to His people, the details about angels they reveal may not be literal. Nonetheless, we see in these visions powerful displays of angels praising the almighty God and Jesus Christ the Lamb.

In the Old Testament there are frequent references to "the angel of the Lord." Many of the Bible passages in this third category clearly describe the One who is over all things including angels. When the angel of the Lord speaks as God Himself in the first person, doing or saying things only God Himself can do or say, it is clearly a manifestation of God Himself, not one of His heavenly creatures. Such theophanies include the angel of the Lord who appears to Hagar (Genesis 16); the angel of the Lord who stopped Abraham from sacrificing Isaac (Genesis 22); the voice that summoned Moses to the burning bush (Exodus 3); God's presence in the pillars of cloud and fire that led Israel out of Egypt (Exodus 14), including the "angel of God" referred to in Exodus 14:19; the angel who blocked the path of Balaam's donkey (Numbers 22); the angel of the Lord who appears to Gideon (Judges 6) and Samson's mother (Judges 13); and the angel who punished God's enemies (2 Chronicles 32).

Because the appearances of this "angel of the Lord" occur only in the Old Testament, some scholars suggest that this might be the preincarnate Christ. In any event, these passages must not be confused with references to God's created heavenly beings—His angels.

A fourth kind of reference to angels is frequently made in the Bible. These are *comments about angels* that describe their work and activity, though angels themselves do not appear. Such references occur in Job 1:6 and 2:1, describing days "the angels came to present themselves before the Lord"; Job 38:7, placing the angels at the creation of the world; Psalm 91:11, reminding us that angels guard and protect God's people; Psalms 103:20 and 148:2, directing the angels to praise God; Matthew 22:30, suggesting that angels do not marry as people do; Matthew 26:53 and several references in Hebrews 1, indicating that Jesus can command the angels to do His will and is superior to them; Paul's comment in 1 Corinthians 6:3 that we will judge angels; and many others.

These references affirm several things for us:
- The existence of angels is confirmed and taken for granted throughout the Bible. The writers of Holy Scripture believed in them and through the writers God communicates about the angels to us.
- Angels have a specific place and purpose in God's kingdom, as we shall see in the study sessions that follow.
- Angels serve God and, by His will, serve and protect us as well.
- Angels, like us, are created beings, but they are not like us. Their nature will be more fully studied in this book.

Throughout this course, keep the Bible study participants mindful of this primary concept—angels are God's messengers. Their words and actions always direct us to God and His great power, glory, and love. Let us never be misled into detached observation of angels as we might study biology or psychology. Nor should we mistake the beauty and power of angels as something independent from God, for that would be idolatry. As we study these amazing servants of God, we will find in them evidence of God's great love for us. Let us hear their proclamations of that love in the birth, passion, and resurrection of Jesus Christ. "A Savior has been born to you" (Luke 2:11); "He is not here; He has risen" (Matthew 28:6); "[He] will come back" (Acts 1:11). All are messages of God's love.

Using This Study with Intergenerational Groups

Adults and youth—parents and their teenagers—can study the Bible together. While that truth should come as no surprise, such study opportunities are rare in most congregations. Recent statistics have shown the power of faith conversations among parents and teens to enhance the spiritual development of teens. Also clear is the need for congregations to assist and support the family in the task of nurturing faith in children and young people (see *Congregations at Crossroads*, © 1995 by Search Institute, pages 21–22).

If you are willing to provide a faith-enhancing opportunity for intergenerational Bible study using this book, keep the following points in mind.
- *Let the voices of youth and adults be heard equally.* Let youth share in oral reading, small-group leadership tasks, and responses to questions as frequently as adults. The young people may initially be somewhat shy. You may occasionally have to encourage or prompt them into greater participation. Adults are often accustomed to group process. You may occasionally have to restrain them by directing questions or appointing roles without waiting for volunteers.
- *Be sensitive to the self-consciousness of some young people.* Especially if intergenerational experiences are new to your congregation, some

young people may be intimidated in groups of adults. Use the warmup activities in this course to "level the playing field" for youth participation.

- *Remember that many adults, as well as young people, are embarrassed to read aloud.* Choose volunteers for such tasks based on your advance knowledge of reading ability or the genuine eagerness of a volunteer to read.

- *Use a variety of group experiences to facilitate interaction.* Build group relationships by moving from activities requiring a low level of self-revelation toward those with greater degrees of intimacy. When creating small groups for discussion and personal sharing, you might start with activities that group adults together and youth together. Mixed groups of four to six, with at least two youth in each group, could follow. The next step could be preliminary discussion in pairs of adults and pairs of youth. Two pairs could then come together (two adults and two youth, preferably not related) for further discussion. For more intimate sharing, pair parents with their teenagers and adults with nonrelated teens.

To facilitate discussion outside of class time between parents and their teens, consider adding a brief discussion assignment to each class to be done as "homework." A starting place for such discussion is provided as Resource Page A. It includes one or more discussion questions related to each of the four sessions in this book. The layout of the page makes it possible for the leader to make a copy for each participating family or individual (plus a few extras) and cut them into smaller slips for distribution at the end of each session.

Discussion Starters

A Note to the leader: Create a copy of this page for each family or individual expected to attend the first session, plus a few extras for others who come only for later sessions. Then cut the pages into smaller slips and distribute one section at the end of each session.

All about **Angels**—Session 1

Discussion Starters

- Where have you seen evidence of society's fascination with angels?
- Rent a movie or identify a television program that features angels. Watch it together and discuss it.

All about **Angels**—Session 2

Discussion Starters

- What surprised you most about the characteristics of angels?
- Share your favorite angel encounter in the Bible and tell why you chose it.

All about **Angels**—Session 3

Discussion Starters

- If you were an angel, what would be your favorite activity or responsibility?
- Share a time when you believed you or someone you loved had been protected by an angel.

All about **Angels**—Session 4

Discussion Starters

- Share a recent time when you sensed Satan tempting you.
- How does it help to know that Jesus has already defeated Satan through His suffering, death, and resurrection when we are tempted to sin?

Angels—Fad or Fact? 1

Focus

Angels are messengers sent from God to believers. The image many people have of angels, though, has been shaped by society, rather than by careful study of God's Word. Through careful study of the Bible, we will discover the truth about angels.

Objectives

That, through the study of God's Word, the participants will
1. recognize angels as servants of God, messengers of His Good News;
2. identify how the Scriptures describe angels;
3. give thanks for God's gracious actions through angels.

Materials Needed

- Bibles
- Pencils or pens
- Copies of Resource Pages 1A–1C (1C is optional)
- Index cards (one per participant)
- Hymnals or songbooks (optional)

Lesson Outline: Angels—Fad or Fact?

Lesson Activity	Minutes	Materials Needed
Warmup Activity (choose one)		
Angels in the News	10	Samples of angel references or pictures in news magazines, newspapers, and other media (optional)
Angelic music	10	Sample recordings of "angel songs" (optional)
A Look at Angels	10	Index cards; pens, pencils, or marking pens
Angel Facts or Fiction	10	Copies of Resource Page 1A
Angels' Appearance	20	Copies of Resource Page 1B, Bibles
Closing Worship	5	Hymnals or songbooks (optional)

Warmup Activity
Angels in the News

Use this activity or the one that follows, but not both, unless you have extra time.

Invite the group to list recent occasions when they have seen angels mentioned or pictured in the media—news magazines, newspapers (including advertisements), television shows (sitcoms and talk shows), and movies. Allow participants to share stories they have heard about angels. As specific examples are mentioned, write them on newsprint or on the board. (If you wish, you may assemble examples before class using recent newspapers and news magazines.)

Unless your group is small, invite the participants to form groups of four or five. Direct them to prepare an answer to this question: "Based on the list we have prepared, what might people today be likely to believe about angels?" If you worked with small groups, allow each group to report its answer.

Angelic Music

Use this activity or the previous one, but not both, unless you have extra time.

Tell the class that, according to one poll, 1 in 10 popular songs in the past 30 years mentions angels (good or evil) in the title or lyrics. Divide the class into groups and have them list as many songs with angels in them as possible in three minutes. *(In a group of young people and their parents, it might be interesting to divide into those two groups for this activity and compare each generation's music.)* When the time is up, ask them to share their list with the group. (You may wish to give a small prize to the group that lists the most songs. You may also wish to plan ahead to locate recordings of such songs and play them for the class.)

A Look at Angels

Distribute index cards and pencils or pens. Ask the participants to picture an angel in their minds. What do they see? Then ask them to draw that image on the index card. (Reassure them that fine art is not required; stick figures will do.)

When everyone appears to be finished, ask them to share their pictures in pairs or, if your group is small enough, share the pictures with the whole group. (In an intergenerational group, use pairs or small groups that include both teens and adults.) After all the pictures have been shared, discuss with the group what characteristics seem to be most common among the pictures. It is likely that such characteristics as round faces, wings, halos, musical instruments, and mouths open in song will be among the most common traits in the pictures. Tell the participants that later in this session they will examine carefully what the Bible says about the outward appearance of angels—what they look like in the eyes of the writers of Holy Scripture.

Alternate activity: With some advance preparation, the leader could gather a variety of angel figurines and angel pictures. Or participants could be asked in advance to bring pictures and figurines to the first class. Display these examples of angels for the class. Then, in small groups or with the whole class, have the participants list the common traits they see.

Angel Facts or Fiction

Distribute copies of Resource Page 1A. Then share with the participants the following paragraph:

"Angels have surged in popularity. Angel memorabilia is a major industry. You can now purchase everything from alligators to zebras with angel wings. Yes, even the kitchen sink is available with angelic faucets! Angels are obviously a topic of high interest these days, but see how well you do on an angel quiz."

Challenge the participants to take the "Angel Facts and Fiction" quiz on the resource page. The answers for the quiz are:

1. 69 percent
2. 32 percent
3. 76 percent
4. *Time, Newsweek, Ladies Home Journal,* and *Redbook* magazines and *USA Today* among others
5. *Touched by an Angel*
6. True (one shopper noted 30 "angel-ware" retail outlets)

Then review the discussion questions on the resource page.

1. Let the participants share their own degree of exposure to this angel frenzy, sharing the things they have seen and their own reactions. If you or other participants have brought examples of angel memorabilia, share them.

2. Answers will vary. Generally speaking, postmodern society exhibits a great openness to spirituality, though not necessarily to traditional Christianity. Angels may appeal to this spiritual interest. When the world threatens our physical safety, guardian angels offer a sense of protection. In a world of materialism and growing secularism, angels may have greater appeal. For some, belief in angels is a substitute for belief in God. For many, belief in angels may offer reassurance in the face of death.

Angels' Appearance

Introduce a preliminary exploration of angels in the Bible by saying, "Along with the popularity of angels has come a quest for the 'truth' about them. Dozens of books offer to reveal their secrets. But only the Bible can give us the real answers for which we search. Angels are mentioned more than 300 times in the Bible, from Genesis to Revelation. Studying these biblical accounts will help us determine what angels really look like.

"Society's image of angels today dates back to the Middle Ages. Until the eighth century, only those commissioned by the church were allowed to write about or draw angels. Then the Second Council of Nicaea in 787 declared it lawful to depict angels in art and literature. The images that were created at that time set the standard for angels in art."

Direct the participants to review the several appearances of angels or angelic beings listed on Resource Page 1B. (In the next session the distinction between cherubim, seraphim, and other angelic beings will be discussed in detail. Most commentators classify the cherubim and seraphim as specific types of angels. For the time being, deal with them as one category.) Remind the participants to develop mental pictures about the things that the Scripture passages describe. (You may wish to assign Bible references to individuals or small groups to review and report information about them. This will be especially helpful in a larger class.) Discuss, using the following information.

- Genesis 19:1–3, 12–17: Scripture is clear that Lot's visitors are angels. It is also apparent that they appeared as men to the other citizens of Sodom. No wings or other extraordinary features are mentioned. In verse 16, Lot and his family were taken *by the hand* by these messengers of Sodom's destruction and led to safety.
- Isaiah 6:1–6: A number of *seraphs* appear to Isaiah in a vision. These angelic beings are mentioned by name only here in Isaiah, but bear resemblance to the "living creatures" in Ezekiel 1 and Revelation 4. Each seraph has six wings, is described with some human features (face and "feet") and sings the praises of God Almighty.
- Daniel 10:4–11: An angel dressed in linen with a "dazzling" appearance—a body like "chrysolite" (a gemstone of great brilliance), a face like lightning, eyes like flaming torches, and arms and legs that gleamed like polished bronze—appears to Daniel in a vision. While the general shape of this angel appears to be human, he possesses an unnatural shine.
- Matthew 28:1–8; John 20:10–13: In two accounts of the resurrection of Jesus, the details differ slightly but have some similarity as well. In Matthew we see an angel roll back the stone that sealed Jesus' tomb, apparently so that the disciples could see for themselves that Jesus was no longer inside; his appearance "was like lightning" and his clothes "were white as snow." In John we see two angels "in white"—apparently the angel had a partner whom Matthew did not report.
- Luke 1:11–20, 26–38; Luke 2:8–15: Three times in Luke's account of Jesus' birth, "an angel of the Lord" appears—to Zechariah, Mary, and the shepherds. Twice he identifies himself as Gabriel; all three times his appearance apparently inspires fear, for he says, "Do not be afraid." No description is provided. The shepherds also see a "great company" of angels who sing God's praises and go "into heaven." Though angels are often depicted flying in the air, none of these biblical descriptions clearly imply such flight. In fact, all these appearances (including the angel "army") would normally involve standing on the ground.
- Revelation 4:6b–8: The living creatures described here in John's vision resemble those in Isaiah and Ezekiel, but they are "covered with eyes." Such a description in John's apocryphal language could be taken symbolically rather than literally.

14

Now invite participants to compare the drawings of angels they prepared at the start of the session with what they have learned in the Bible passages. Did their angel pictures have wings? halos? human form?

Discuss the questions at the bottom of the resource page, incorporating the following information:

1. No. Angel appearances that are not in visions have no specific references to wings or flying. Explain that artists in the Middle Ages had limited access to copies of the Bible and often created their images of angels by embellishing on what they had heard and remembered. They took the images of the Greek gods and goddesses (who were also messengers) and added wings to them to show swiftness. The wings were generally modeled after those of two noble birds: the eagle (with wings outstretched on either side) or the swan (with wings partially "nested" in a heart shape).

2. A *halo* is defined as "an aura of glory, veneration, or sentiment surrounding an idealized person or thing" (Webster's Tenth Collegiate). Many of the angel descriptions in the Bible refer to great brilliance, often associated with the glory of the Lord. Artists used halos to represent this supernatural aura. Early artwork depicted Jesus and Mary with halos to set them apart from others in the paintings. A similar artistic convention was employed in depicting angels. It may be that since church laws said artists had to use real gold leaf in painting auras, and it was too expensive for artists to draw a whole aura of light, they drew only halos.

3. Angels can and do take on human form, but are not always described in that way. Explain that angels can apparently take on human form when necessary. They can also be invisible to the human eye (see Numbers 22:21–34) or have animal features (Ezekiel 1:14). Sometimes angels are described in the Bible as "flames of fire" (Psalm 104:4). People who have had angel experiences say angels can also materialize in the form of a mist or a light. Others describe angels like a light that fills the room, "magic dust," a sunrise in brilliant blues with glitter, or a shimmering mother of pearl. Angels are *spirits*, not humans. We must be careful of extremes.

4. Answers will vary. The traditional wings shown on angels are certainly not universal in the Bible's angel descriptions.

5. Generally speaking, angel images of today seem to lack the power and mystery of angels. The winged toddlers (like our image of the Greek god Cupid) are especially difficult to support. The participants will notice other similarities and differences.

Closing Worship

Sing the hymn "It Came Upon the Midnight Clear," found in most hymnals and Christmas songbooks. If time permits, discuss the appearance of, and communication methods used by, angels in this hymn.

End the session with a prayer like this one: "Dear Lord, creator of the angels, thank You for the precious gift of Your holy angels. Help us to seek the truth about angels in Your Word, rather than in the images given to us by the world. In Jesus' name we pray. Amen."

Extending the Lesson

Use the following questions as alternatives for or extensions of the lesson activities.

1. Draw a second picture of an angel based on what you learned today. How does this image compare with your first drawing?

2. Distribute copies of "How Do Angels Communicate?" (Resource Page 1C). Invite participants to complete the page alone or in pairs. When most are finished, review the discussion questions on this page.

In Revelation 8:2 and following, seven angels blow trumpets to begin a series of plagues. This could tell us where the music legend comes from. Angels frequently are described singing their praises to God. In addition it is their honored task to share the best news in all the world—news of a Savior who was born in Bethlehem, suffered to pay for our sins, and rose again to guarantee us new life now and eternally. Who wouldn't laugh and sing for joy?

Angel Facts and Fiction

① What percentage of Americans say they believe in **Angels**?
- a. 69 percent
- b. 57 percent
- c. 49 percent
- d. 74 percent

② Of that number, how many claim to have had some type of **Angel** experience?
- a. 52 percent
- b. 62 percent
- c. 25 percent
- d. 32 percent

③ What percentage of teenagers (according to a 1992 Gallup Poll) also believe in **Angels**?
- a. 86 percent
- b. 76 percent
- c. 66 percent
- d. 36 percent

④ In the past five years **Angels** have been featured in what national periodicals?

⑤ Recently **Angels** have been the subject of TV documentaries and what popular series?

⑥ True or false? Entire stores in some shopping malls and many catalog outlets are devoted entirely to **Angel** merchandise.

Questions for discussion:

1. Which of the many print, TV, or retail "angel encounters" have you seen personally?

2. What do you think accounts for the renewed interest in angels?

Angels' Appearance

Read the Bible passages and note their descriptions of angels. As you read, try to picture each event in your mind.

- Genesis 19:1–3, 12–17
- Isaiah 6:1–6
- Ezekiel 1:1–14
- Daniel 10:4–11
- Matthew 28:1–8; John 20:10–13
- Luke 1:11–20, 26–38; Luke 2:8–15
- Revelation 4:6b–8

Questions for discussion:

1. Do all the angels in Scripture have wings? Why do you think most artistic representations of angels indicate wings?
2. What is a halo? Why do you think artists drew halos on angel pictures?
3. Do all angels in Scripture appear in human form? Why do you think some appear to be human and some do not? How would you expect an angel to appear?
4. Why do you think society has a concept of angels largely unchanged since the Middle Ages? What do you think could be done to change these images?
5. How does the Bible's image of angels differ from the figurines in the stores? In what ways are they the same?

How Do Angels Communicate?

- In 1 Corinthians 13:1, Paul writes, "If I speak in the tongues of men *and of angels*, but have not love, I am only a resounding gong or a clanging symbol." This seems to imply an angelic language. Do you think that angels have a language of their own? Why or why not?

- Legends say that music and laughter are the language of angels. Why are these forms of communication appropriate for angels?

The word that the Bible translates as "angel"—both in the Greek and the Hebrew—means "messenger." Angels' main functions are to praise God and to bring messages from God to us. How they deliver those messages is not nearly as important as the fact that they deliver them.

All about **Angels**

What Are Angels Like? 2

Focus

Angels are created, personal beings, but they are not people. God gives them some supernatural powers, but they also have limitations. Angels should not be worshiped or prayed to; our prayers and worship belong only to God.

Objectives

That, through the study of God's Word, the participants will
1. understand that angels were created by the triune God;
2. recognize that angels are personal beings with both supernatural powers and limitations;
3. remember that angels are not to be worshiped, but that they serve and point us to God, who alone is worthy of all our praise.

Materials Needed

- Bibles
- Pencils or pens
- Copies of Resource Pages 2A–2C (2C is optional)
- Blank paper
- Hymnals or songbooks (optional)

Lesson Outline: What Are Angels Like?

Lesson Activity	Minutes	Materials Needed
Warmup Activity	10	
Angels—Created, Personal Beings	20	Copies of Resource Page 2A, Bibles
Angel Categories	5	Bibles, chalkboard and chalk or marker board and markers
Powers and Limitations	15	Copies of Resource Page 2B, Bibles
Closing Worship	5	Hymnals or songbooks (optional)

Warmup Activity

Make sure each participant has blank paper and a pencil or pen. Challenge the participants to create a list of all the angels who are called by name in the Bible. Allow about three minutes for this activity. Then invite participants to name angels.

(As an alternative, you could establish two or more teams. In a class of teenagers and adults, you may wish to let adults compete with teens.)

Only three angel names are listed in Scripture—Michael (Daniel 10:13; Jude 9; and Revelation 12:7); Gabriel (Luke 1:19, 26); and Lucifer (Isaiah 14:12 in some translations; also called Satan in Job 1:6 and other passages). No others are referred to by name. (No, "Lo, an angel of the Lord" and "Hark, the herald angel" are not biblical angel names.) Some participants may mention names such as Raphael, Uriel, and others that are listed in the Apocrypha. These texts are part of the Roman Catholic Bible but are not accepted as divinely inspired books of the Bible by most churches.

Angels—Created, Personal Beings

Distribute copies of "Angels—Created, Personal Beings" (Resource Page 2A). Read, or invite a volunteer to read, the opening paragraph. Then ask the participants, "Where did angels come from?" Accept all responses. Some may have the mistaken notion that we become angels when we die. Ask, "Why might people have that impression?" Challenge the participants to identify where people may have picked up certain ideas about the origin of angels. (Some incorrectly interpret Jesus' statement, "I have other sheep that are not of this sheep pen" [John 10:16] to mean angels. Cartoons have often depicted death as the time when the soul leaves the body as an angel with wings. This may have come from cartoons drawn during the Black Plague. The newspapers put cartoons of baby spirits rising from their dead bodies in angelic form. They termed these spirits "Cherubs," because of the reference in Matthew 18:10 that children's angels always behold the face of the Father. Only the cherubim and the seraphim were thought to reside in God's presence at all times. Others may confuse the idea of being *with* the angels in heaven after the last day with *being* angels. Movies and television shows frequently offer information about angels that is not biblical.)

Lead into the resource page by saying, "If we do not become angels when we die, how do angels come into being? Let's take a look at the origin and nature of these servants of God." If your class is small, you may be able to work through the resource page together. With a group of eight or more participants, you may wish to divide into smaller groups for study and discussion. If so, use the comments below to review the small-group discussion with the whole class.

1. The psalmist, inspired by God, includes angels in the list of created things. Angels did not exist from eternity as God did, but are created beings. Paul, reaffirming the createdness of angels, writes: "By Him [that

is, Christ] all things were created: things in heaven and on earth, visible and invisible … all things were created by Him and for Him." We can safely say that angels were created at some point in the six days of creation. God's description of creation in Job 38:7 ("while the morning stars sang together and all the angels shouted for joy") describes angels as witnesses to the creation. For this reason, although the Bible does not specifically list angels in the creation account, it is thought that angels were created on the first day when God created the "heavens and the earth" (Genesis 1:1).

The language used to describe the number of angels ("thousands upon thousands … ten thousand times ten thousand") seems to describe a countless number. The Talmud suggests that every Jew has 11,000 guardian angels assigned at birth—that's a lot of angels! (Malcomb Godwin, *Angels, an Endangered Species*, page 69.)

2. Mark 12:25 and Luke 20:36 say that we will be "like the angels" (not that we *become* angels), who neither marry nor grow old and die. Logic tells us that angels then do not have children as we do. They have no families, ancestors, or babies. Their number would seem to be the same today as when God created them.

3. Among the personal characteristics in angels that the Bible describes are the emotions of joy (at the creation in Job 38:7 and at the salvation of sinners in Luke 15:10); sorrow or compassion (in Zechariah 1:12–13 the interpreting angel is comforted by the LORD); and fury (ascribed to the devil, a fallen angel, in Revelation 12:12). A woman whose words God causes to be recorded in 2 Samuel 14:19 credits David with "wisdom like that of an angel of God." 2 Peter 2:4 makes it clear that angels had a moral will and were capable of sin.

4. The Bible shows some angels to be individuals with names and voices who appear in a personal form and speak for God with independent voices. It is clear that while angels are not like us in many ways, as we shall further see, they have many traits with which we can identify.

Angel Categories

On the board or on newsprint write these three terms: *cherubim, seraphim,* and *archangels.* Invite participants to recall, if they can, examples of each from the Bible passages they have looked at so far in this course. Discuss each term, using the information below to inform your discussion.

The *cherubim* are pictured in Scripture in Genesis 3:24 and Ezekiel (mentioned by name and also called "living creatures" in the early chapters of the book). They are four in number and described by Ezekiel as having four wings and four faces (man, lion, ox, and eagle). They are depicted as throne attendants and decorate the ark of the covenant (Exodus 25:18– 20), are embroidered on the 10 curtains of the tabernacle (Exodus 26:1), and later decorated the temple in Jerusalem, both as huge carved statues and as images carved into the woodwork. In this way the cherubim attended the earthly thrones of God, just as they attend His throne in heaven. Point out that these *cherubs* are quite unlike "cherubs" we might see in Renaissance pictures and children's choirs.

The *seraphim* (or *seraphs*) are mentioned by name only in Isaiah 6. They are described by Isaiah as having six wings. With two wings they flew and with the others they covered themselves—two wings covering their faces and two covering their feet. Isaiah does not count the seraphs for us but uses the plural indicating many. The seraphs bear considerable resemblance to the "living creatures" that later appear in the book of Revelation. Like the cherubim, the seraphs are strongly associated with the throne of God and serve in His heavenly realm.

These two distinct types of angelic beings are distinguished from other angels that appear in the Bible in that they are generally seen in visions. They seem to be different from the angel messengers who frequently appear in a personal way to God's people in other sections of the Bible.

Archangels, or chief princes (as Michael is called in Daniel 10:13), seem to be a leading rank of God's angel messengers. They are mentioned by name only in 1 Thessalonians 4:16 and Jude 9. In the early days of the Christian church, angels were divided into a divine order of societies or "choirs." One such division included seraphim, cherubim, watchers, thrones, dominions, virtues, powers, principalities, archangels, and angels (based on Romans 8:38 and other verses). Such hierarchies were accepted by the church until the Reformation in the 16th century when Martin Luther swept aside this notion as unscriptural. He saw people putting too much emphasis on angels and not enough emphasis on God.

Powers and Limitations

Distribute copies of "Powers and Limitations" (Resource Page 2B). Ask for a volunteer to read the opening paragraph. Talk about the powers that Superman and other super heroes possess and the limits to their powers. (Superman possessed the normal characteristics of people from his world, Krypton, but on our world exceeded the abilities of humans by considerable magnitude. Another person from Krypton would be his equal in our world. His powers—indeed, his very life force—were inhibited by the radiation of kryptonite. In its presence Superman became weak and would eventually die.) Alert the participants that angels have similar powers and limitations.

Direct the participants to the Bible references on the resource page. Invite them—alone, in pairs, or in small groups—to check each reference and place it in the appropriate column on the resource page with a few words describing the power or limitation it describes. *You may wish to assign just one or two references to each individual or group to complete on behalf of the group.*

1. Supernatural powers: 2 Samuel 24:15–16 (God uses an angel to spread a plague across Israel); Daniel 3:24–29 (an angel appears in the blazing furnace with the three young men, is not burned, and protects them from the flames); Daniel 6:22 (an angel protects Daniel from the hungry lions); Acts 12:6–10 (an angel rescues Peter from prison, appearing inside the prison, removing his chains, and causing the prison gates to

open by themselves); Revelation 18:21 (in John's vision an angel shows tremendous strength).

2. Limitations: Matthew 8:28–29 (angels' strength is limited—these demons [evil angels] acknowledge their inferiority to Jesus); Matthew 24:36 (angels' knowledge is limited); Luke 1:26 (angels obey God's commands); Revelation 22:8–9 (angels are not worthy of our worship).

As you review these last two passages—Luke 1:26 and Revelation 22:8–9—emphasize that God is more powerful than any angel. He created the angels to serve Him and all they do is at His command and as an extension of His power. The angels themselves make it clear that we are not to pray to them (Revelation 22:8–9) or worship them in any way. Such a practice would be idolatry, violating the First Commandment—worshiping the things God has created rather than God Himself.

Closing Worship

End the session with the following prayer: "Christ Jesus, You were there when the angels were created. You know them by name as You know each one of us by name. Thank You for these wonders of Your creation and for guiding them in Your service. Keep us mindful of the fact that they have limitations as well as powers, so that our worship and prayers are always directed to You. We ask it in Jesus' name. Amen."

You may wish to read or sing two or more stanzas of "All Creatures of Our God and King," especially stanzas 1 and 7.

Extending the Lesson

1. An Angel Story

Read, or invite a volunteer to read, "An Angel Story," Resource Page 2C, aloud. *(You may wish to copy the page so that each of the participants can follow along.)*

After the story has been read, briefly discuss the following questions.

1. What must the villain in Mr. Jahn's story have seen to frighten him away so thoroughly? (The sight of an "angel guard" composed of many angels was apparently quite impressive. It would seem that the ex-convict recognized the extraordinary power of those that protected Mr. Jahn's father.)

2. What powers of angels are suggested in the story? (The angels were invisible to one man but visible to another at the same time. They also knew in advance of the man's danger and came to protect him, even before he prayed to God.

3. What are the implications of Psalm 34:7: "The angel of the LORD encamps around those who fear Him, and He delivers them"? (Unlike the fear of the ex-convict, the psalmist promises God's protection to those who fear the LORD, that is, those who believe in His great power and trust in Him for their life and salvation.)

2. Judging the Angels?

In 1 Corinthians 6:3 Paul tells the Corinthian Christians that they will judge the angels—"Do you not know that we will judge angels? How much more the things of this life!" Discuss this somewhat puzzling statement with the class. 2 Peter 2:4 and 9, and Jude 6, clearly indicate that like all people, the fallen angels will be subject to judgment on the Last Day. Scripture is not clear about how Christians will be involved in this judgment. (This passing comment by Paul is not the main point of his comments to the Corinthians. He encourages them to settle their disputes among themselves without resort to the worldly courts, relying on God's Law and Gospel as it is revealed in the Scriptures.) While these passages seem to indicate that we will have some authority over the fallen angels, no ranking of God's created beings can be assumed.

Angels—Created, Personal Beings

The young lady pictured below is confused. Will an angel outfit be waiting for her in heaven? No, because angels are angels and people are people, even in heaven. People don't become angels when they die.

Where did angels come from? What are they like? Given the many misconceptions present in television shows and movies, these are important questions. Study the following Bible passages. Locate and summarize the information that relates to each characteristic of angels listed below.

1. Angels were created by God during the six days of creation (Psalm 148:1–5; Colossians 1:15–16), in great number (Deuteronomy 33:2; Daniel 7:10; Hebrews 12:22).

2. Do angels have babies? families? ancestors? Do they grow old and die? Check out what Jesus says in Mark 12:25 and Luke 20:36.

3. However, angels do have many characteristics of personal beings:
   - Emotions—Job 38:7; Luke 15:10; Zechariah 1:12–13; Revelation 12:12
   - Intelligence—2 Samuel 14:20
   - Moral will—2 Peter 2:4

4. The Bible identifies some angels by name (Daniel 10:13; Jude 9; Revelation 12:7; and Luke 1:19, 26), further evidence of their individuality and personal character. They have a sense of personal identity (as when Gabriel identifies himself by name to Zechariah) even as they serve the One who created them at the beginning of the world.

Powers and Limitations

Angels possess supernatural powers, given to them by God. Cartoon characters have been modeled after the archangel Michael and other mighty angels. Superman and other "super heroes" are examples. Just as Superman battles the forces of evil in the world of animation, God's angel hosts are at war with the forces of evil in our world. And just as Superman has limitations to his powers, the power of angels is also limited. Identify the supernatural powers or limitations of angels in each passage below. Write the Bible reference and a brief description of the power or limitation in the appropriate column in the chart.

	Powers	Limitations
2 Samuel 24:15–16		
Daniel 3:24–29		
Daniel 6:22		
Matthew 8:28–29		
Matthew 24:36		
Luke 1:26		
Acts 12:6–10		
Revelation 18:21		
Revelation 22:8–9		

An Angel Story

(as told by Richard C. Jahn in *Abiding Word*, volume 3, © CPH 1960)

" My sainted father was the pastor of a congregation in western Nebraska near Fort Kearney. It became necessary for him to take a firm stand against an utterly depraved man. Chiefly because of the testimony of my father, this man was convicted and sentenced to several years of hard labor. This criminal is the only person that I ever personally saw wear a ball and chain. He was filled with bitter, vindictive hatred against my father and vowed that he would kill him.

"On one occasion after the man's release, my father was walking the streets of Fort Kearney late one night and when he approached a certain alley, he heard footsteps all around him. He looked in every direction; there was enough light that he could see quite well, but he could see no people at all. When he would stop, there was no sound. When he moved forward, he again could hear these footsteps all about him. In his apprehension he prayed to the Lord for protection against any evil that might threaten to harm him, but the footsteps kept right on.

"Finally, as Father crossed an alley, the ex-convict sprang at him, brandishing a club, but before he could take more than

a step, an expression of utter fright came upon his face. He dropped the club and ran down the alley, screaming, and my father never saw him again. After he had crossed the alley, the footsteps ceased, and he never heard them any more.

"He always believed, and used to tell us children, that he was convinced that the Lord had sent a guard of angels, invisible to him, but visible to the would-be assassin, that protected him on that night. "

What Do Angels Do? 3

Focus

God has given His angels specific purposes, duties, and responsibilities. They worship God in ceaseless praise and seek to carry out His commands. They minister to Christians by watching over us. They bring messages from God to His people. The angels performed special functions at the first coming of Christ and will be present when He returns in glory.

Objectives

That, through the study of God's Word, the participants will
1. identify ways that angels carry out God's commands;
2. recognize the unique ministry of the angels in the life of Christ and in His return;
3. see God's grace at work in their own lives, possibly through the ministry of His angels.

Materials Needed

- Bibles
- Pencils or pens
- Copies of Resource Pages 3A–3E (3E is optional)
- Hymnals or songbooks (optional)

Lesson Outline: What Do Angels Do?

Lesson Activity	Minutes	Materials Needed
Warmup Activity (choose one)		
Who's Greater?	5	
Angel Activity Charades	10	
Angels and Other Faiths	10	Copies of Resource Page 3A
Angels and God Almighty	10	Copies of Resource Page 3B, Bibles
Angels and Us	10	Copies of Resource Page 3C, Bibles
Angels in the Life of Jesus	10	Copies of Resource Page 3D, Bibles
Closing Worship	5	Hymnals or songbooks (optional)

Warmup Activity

Who's Greater?

Use this activity or the one that follows, but not both, unless you have extra time.

Invite the participants to react to the following pairs of people, choosing the greater role in each. Have them signal their choices in a way that will work with your group: raising hands or moving to a specific location in the room. Accept all opinions, but, after each vote, briefly discuss the choices made and the reasoning behind them.

the athlete	or	the coach?
the accountant	or	the CFO (chief financial officer)?
the letter writer	or	the mail carrier?
the composer	or	the musician?
the doctor	or	the scalpel?
the architect	or	the bricklayer?
the teacher	or	the student?
the general	or	the pilot who executes the general's orders?
the chef	or	the server who brings the food?
the judge	or	the jailer who carries out the sentence?

Point out that in some cases it may be hard to decide who is more important. However, in the case of God and His angels, the angel is never more important than God, who directs the angels in their tasks. Our worship, our prayers, and our confidence in divine support must always be directed to God Almighty.

Angel Activity Charades

Use this activity or the previous one, but not both, unless you have extra time.

Before class write a number of angel activities on separate index cards or scraps of paper. Include activities such as an angel warning someone not to go a certain place, an angel announcing good news, an angel punishing evil-doers, or an angel praising God. Give the activity descriptions to pairs of participants and, after a few moments for preparation, invite the pairs to act out the activity silently for the rest of the class. Challenge the class to guess the activity.

If you are teaching a group of youth and adults together, this would be a good activity to keep youth and parents together, or to pair a young person and adult. If the numbers of youth and adults are not even, use some groups of three with at least one youth and one adult in each.

After the charades have been identified, point out that God has given His angels many different kinds of tasks, but they are all done at His direction and for His purposes. This study will focus on these angel activities.

Angels and Other Faiths

Begin the study by saying, "Belief in angels is not exclusive to Christianity. All the major world religions profess such a belief. Just as there are false gods, there may be false angels. We can identify those things that are godly, including the activity of angels, through the study of God's Word, the Bible."

Distribute copies of "Angels and Other Faiths" (Resource Page 3A). Read aloud, or ask a volunteer to read aloud, the opening paragraph. Then ask for volunteers to read what each religion believes about angels. Invite participants to share their reactions to the different beliefs.

You may wish to assign each paragraph to one-third of the participants to discuss in small groups. Then let each group report to the whole class. Additional reference books might be helpful, if you have additional time.

Then discuss the questions on the resource page with the class. Use these suggested responses to guide the discussion.

1. Why is it important to know that belief in angels is not exclusive to Christianity? Do you think real angels could mislead people into non-Christian beliefs and practices? (Not all angels serve the one, true God. The Bible calls Satan the father of lies [John 8:44]. Angels who serve God will act in ways and bring messages that are consistent with His Word and will.)

2. How can understanding what others believe about angels help us as Christians? (It makes us more alert to the possible presence of angels in our own lives. It also helps us to be prepared to witness to others about our own faith when the opportunity arises.)

Angels and God Almighty

Distribute copies of "Angels and God Almighty" (Resource Page 3B). Assign each Bible passage on the resource page to a participant. After a few moments let the participants gather in small groups according to how the passages are grouped on the resource page to discuss the angel duties described. *If your class is small, assign each group to a participant, or study all the passages together, doing just one or two in each group as you have time.*

After allowing the groups a few moments for discussion, review each section of the resource page, allowing volunteers to describe the angels' duties they observed. (In the first passages, angels *forewarn* God's people about coming dangers; in the second, they *execute God's judgment* on people; in the third, angels *worship* God; and in the last group they *protect and rescue* God's people from harm threatened by others.) Then discuss the questions on the resource page, using the following information.

1. The categories in these questions are not identical to those on the resource page. Genesis 19:11–13 and Matthew 2:13, 19–20 correspond roughly to (a) and (b); Genesis 3:24, 2 Samuel 24:15–17, and Matthew 13:41–42 and 49–50 describe God executing judgment through His angels (c); Isaiah 6:1–8 and Revelation 7:11–12 describe angels praising God, an activity that is not included in this question; and Daniel 6:22 and Acts 5:19 illustrate a kind of providential intervention by God (d). There are many other ways in which the activities could be grouped.

2. Answers to this question will vary. Stress that today we have God's Word, from which we draw His messages for our lives, and His Spirit, who guides us "into all truth" (John 16:13). An important reminder for us is that the angels appear to be in constant obedience and praise of God. Their example can encourage us in our own Spirit-led lives of worship and service.

Angels and Us

Distribute copies of Resource Page 3C. Request that the participants work through the four angel activities on the resource page individually to discover how angels have served God's people in the past. After most participants have finished, call the group together. Ask them to share what they learned. Suggested responses include the following:

1. Angels *rescued Peter.*
2. Angels *provided knowledge of the future to Paul.*
3. Angels *guarded God's people.*
4. Angels *announced the Good News of Jesus' birth and resurrection.*

Angels guard us, protect us, meet our physical and emotional needs, and deliver messages from God to us. Discuss the questions on the resource page with the group, using the following information.

1. It will be evident that not everyone recognizes angels at work in their lives. God has and uses other means to provide all that we need. He does not *have* to use angels, though surely He can if He chooses. No other judgment can safely be made about those who have not experienced angels than that God may not have chosen for them to do so. On the other hand, angel activities have been reported by many of God's people, and it would seem foolish to deny that they exist and continue to be available to do His will.

2. Knowing the many ways they can serve may help us be alert to God's goodness in our lives, whether it comes through angels or through another channel.

3. The concept of personal guardian angels is a popular one, neither conclusively taught nor opposed in the Bible. That angel guardians are *available* to God's people is clear, however.

Conclude this section of the study by reading the "Important Point" at the bottom of the resource page.

If you have extra time at this point, you may wish to use the Extending the Lesson activity on evaluating angel experiences.

Angels in the Life of Jesus

Distribute copies of "Angels in the Life of Jesus" (Resource Page 3D). Divide the participants into four groups. Assign one group the birth of Christ, one group His life on earth, the third group His death and resurrection, and the fourth group the Second Coming. Ask them to fill out the portion of the box that describes their assignment. *If your group is small, work through each box with the entire class, or assign just one or two people to each box.*

After five minutes, ask for reports on each section. Many of the Bible passages will be familiar by now and will not require much time to digest. Gabriel announced the birth of Jesus to Mary and the shepherds, and the angel host sang praises. An angel appeared to Joseph to reassure him about his approaching marriage to Mary, to the Wise Men as they traveled to and from Bethlehem, and came to strengthen Jesus after His temptation in the wilderness. An angel assisted Jesus again as He prayed in the garden. An angel announced Jesus' resurrection from death and cheered up the disciples after His ascension. And the angels will announce His Second Coming with trumpets, help execute the final events of this age, and gather all people for judgment on the Last Day. What a privilege they have to serve Him! They are truly angels—"messengers" of God's grace—as they witness, and share with us, the salvation God works for us through the life, suffering, death, and resurrection of His Son, our Lord Jesus Christ.

Remind the participants as you conclude this session that the angels function only according to God's will—never according to our desires. Their service cannot be expected or demanded. Like all of God's gracious gifts, the angels serve to point us to God, to whom we owe all thanks and praise.

Closing Worship

Conclude with this prayer: "Thank You, heavenly Father, for sending Your angels to serve Your people—even as they serve You and Your Son, Jesus. Give us patience as we wait for the Second Coming when Jesus will appear with all His angels. In His name we pray. Amen."

You may wish to close with the hymn "Ye Watchers and Ye Holy Ones," found in most hymnals.

Extending the Lesson

Testing the Spirits

Distribute copies of "Testing the Spirits" (Resource Page 3E). Ask the participants to share stories of angel experiences they have heard or read about (or use one of the stories below). Use the questions on the resource page to evaluate the experience.

1. Jan's story: "Several years ago, I was in the hospital, scheduled to have heart surgery. I was so afraid. I worried about my family and how they were dealing with the possibility of my death. I prayed for comfort. That evening, a nurse came and sat by my bed. She told me that everything was going to be okay, and I believed her. I felt this immense peace come over me. The next morning, I asked another nurse if she could tell the nurse who sat with me how grateful I was. She looked at me in a strange way and told me she was the only nurse on duty that night. I praised God for answering my prayer."

2. Dave's story: "I woke up in the night to get a drink of water and saw this person (I don't remember if it was male or female) sitting on the bed next to me. I asked this person what they were doing there and got no response, so I went to the bathroom and got a drink. When I came back, it was gone. Was this an angel?"

3. John's story: "When I was five years old, I was standing at the top of a steep staircase. The door to the staircase opened and I fell to the bottom of the stairs. At the bottom, an angel caught me. My mother saw me suspended in the air but did not see the angel. It was a beautiful creature of light. I was not afraid. I thank God for providing me with this protection." (John is now 70 years old.)

Angels and Other Faiths

Belief in angels is not exclusive to the Christian religion. Almost all major world religions believe in some form of angels. Among them are these:

Judaism: Many references to angels are found in the Jewish scriptures—the Talmud and the Torah. According to the Talmud, each Jewish person is assigned 11,000 guardian angels at birth. (Malcomb Godwin, *Angels, an Endangered Species*, page 69.)

Islam: The prophet Muhammad claimed that the angel Gabriel dictated the Qur'an to him. Muslims believe that everyone is assigned two recording angels at birth. One records a person's good deeds; one records a person's evil deeds. At the end of life, the lists are compared to determine where that person will spend eternity. Islamic tradition also says that there is an angel in every raindrop.

Mormonism: The Church of Jesus Christ of Latter-day Saints teaches that their founder, Joseph Smith, was guided by an angel named Moroni to gold plates that Smith transcribed into the *Book of Mormon.*

Discuss the following:

1. Why is it important to know that belief in angels is not exclusive to Christianity? Do you think real angels could mislead people into non-Christian beliefs and practices?

2. How can understanding what others believe about angels help us as Christians?

Angels and God Almighty

From one perspective, angels are servants of God. They act according to His will and directions. Read the following Bible passages and list the duties of the angels in each group of passages.

- Genesis 19:11–13; Matthew 2:13, 19–20

- Genesis 3:24; 2 Samuel 24:15–17; Matthew 13:41–42, 49–50

- Isaiah 6:1–8; Revelation 7:11–12

- Daniel 6:22; Acts 5:19

To Do

☑ Guard Eden
☑ Announce Jesus' birth
☑ Wait for John and Peter at the tomb
☐ Choir practice
☑ Guard Jimmy during bike ride
☐ Last Day roundup

Discuss the following:

1. One writer identifies four categories of angel activity: (a) conveying messages from God to people; (b) foretelling special acts of God; (c) serving as agents of divine judgment; and (d) serving as agents of divine providence. How well do these categories match up with the Bible references above?

2. What strikes you as most interesting or important among the various activities of angels?

Angels and Us

There is also a human perspective to the service of angels—they are involved in the lives of God's people. God sent angels to minister to us. Read the following Scripture passages to discover what angels can do for you. Be aware of how the potential for this angelic service makes you feel.

1. Angels _____. (Acts 12:5–11)
2. Angels _____. (Acts 27:23–26)
3. Angels _____. (Psalm 91:11; 2 Kings 6:14–17)
4. Angels _____. (Luke 1:26–38; Matthew 28:1–7)

Discuss these questions:

1. On a scale of one to five, with one being low, how aware are you of the work of angels in your life? Why might some people never sense the work of angels?

2. Why is it important for us to study these holy creatures? What can we gain from knowing about their many ways of service?

3. Do you think you have a guardian angel? (Remember the angel guards in Psalm 91:11–12; Daniel 6:22; Matthew 18:10.)

An important point to remember: Angels intervene according to God's will, not ours. We do not go to angels with prayers for assistance, but we pray to *God*, who created and still directs them.

Angels in the Life of Jesus

Angels were active in every aspect of Jesus' life. Summarize below how angels participated in the ministry of Jesus.

① **Christ's Birth**—Luke 1:26–38; 2:1–40

② **His Life on Earth**—Matthew 1:20–21; 2:13–23; 4:6–11

③ **His Death and Resurrection**—Luke 22:39–44; Matthew 28:1–7; Acts 1:9–11

④ **The Second Coming**—Revelation 10:7; 11:15; 14:6–7 (and many other portions of this book), and Matthew 24:31

 All about **Angels**

Testing the Spirits

How can you tell if an angel experience is real? Use the criteria below.

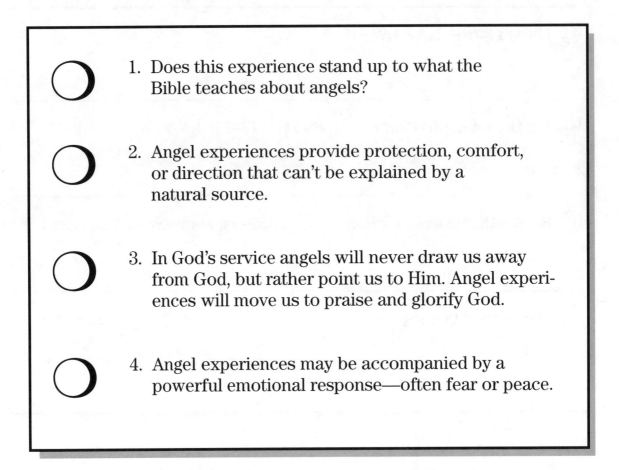

1. Does this experience stand up to what the Bible teaches about angels?

2. Angel experiences provide protection, comfort, or direction that can't be explained by a natural source.

3. In God's service angels will never draw us away from God, but rather point us to Him. Angel experiences will move us to praise and glorify God.

4. Angel experiences may be accompanied by a powerful emotional response—often fear or peace.

Remember that it is our responsibility to "*test* the spirits," not merely *trust* the spirits. Test the spirits against the Word of God (1 John 4:1–6). "The one who is in you is greater than the one who is in the world" (1 John 4:4).

Angels—Evil and Good 4

Focus

The Bible reveals evil angels, or demons, at war with God and His people. Angels, like all creation, were created good. But some angels rebelled against God, were banished from heaven, and now oppose Him. God arms us for spiritual warfare, defends us against attacks of Satan, and has guaranteed the final victory for us by the death and resurrection of His Son.

Objectives

That, through the study of God's Word, the participants will

1. recognize that angel references in the Bible can be to good angels, evil angels (demons), and to God Himself;
2. be aware of the threat posed by Satan and evil angels;
3. know that, through faith and by God's grace, they can stand firm against all evil;
4. rejoice in the final victory over Satan, sin, and death, which is theirs through faith in Jesus Christ.

Materials Needed

- Bibles
- Pencils or pens
- Copies of Resource Pages 4A–4C
- Art supplies or craft materials (optional)
- Hymnals or songbooks (optional)

Lesson Outline: Angels—Evil and Good

Lesson Activity	Minutes	Materials Needed
Warmup Activity	10	Chalkboard and chalk or newsprint and marking pens (optional)
Satan and His Kingdom	15	Copies of Resource Page 4A, Bibles
The Angel of the LORD	10	Copies of Resource Page 4B, Bibles
God's Final Victory	15	Art supplies, craft materials, or copies of Resource Page 4C, Bibles
Closing Worship	5	Hymnals or songbooks (optional)

Advance Preparation

In the concluding activity, participants will be invited to recreate a portion of John's vision of heaven. To enhance this activity assemble art materials (marking pens or paints, large pieces of suitable paper, wallpaper samples, foil paper, construction paper, and glue) or craft materials (cardboard, clay, foam balls, foil, pipe cleaners, and the like) with which they can work. If you are unable to assemble such material, Resource Page 4C can be copied for each participant and used instead.

Warmup Activity

Divide the class into pairs. Have Person A in each pair sit facing away from you. Then write the word "Satan" in large letters on the board or on a piece of paper for Person B in each pair to see. When you say "Begin," Person B should describe Satan to Person A *without using Satan's name*, only physical characteristics. The first pair in which Person A correctly guesses who is being described wins.

As an alternate activity, use two groups (intergenerational groups might divide into youth and adults). Each group should appoint an artist to draw for their group. Each artist is given a marker or chalk and a writing surface. Everyone but the artist is allowed to see the name "Satan." At your signal, each group seeks to communicate to their artist how to illustrate Satan. After two or three minutes, the group with the best picture wins.

Then ask the group, "Do you really think Satan looks that way? How might he appear if we were to see him today? Why do we still think of him in such an outlandish way (horns, pointed tail, red suit or skin, etc.)? Do we expect Satan and his work to be easier to recognize than that of good angels?" Answers to these questions will vary. The goal is to help the group focus and get them talking.

Emphasize to the participants that Satan was a good angel at one time and probably looks the same as the other angels in the Bible. In our world, Satan tries to deceive us by presenting himself in an appealing manner. If he looked scary, it would be easy to run away from him!

Point out to the class that today's session will investigate what the Bible says about Satan and how to resist Him. It will also explore references in the Old Testament to "the angel of the LORD" and God's final victory over Satan.

Satan and His Kingdom

Distribute copies of "Satan and His Kingdom" (Resource Page 4A). Read aloud, or ask a volunteer to read aloud, the opening paragraph. Review briefly these points about Satan and the other fallen angels:
* It is apparent that some of God's angels were unfaithful and were therefore cast out of heaven (see Isaiah 14:12–15; 2 Peter 2:4; and Jude 6).

- This seems likely to have taken place between the beginning of creation and the events of Genesis 3 (when Satan, one of the fallen angels, tempts Adam and Eve in the form of a serpent).

Together look up the Bible passages and record what they say about the worldly kingdom of Satan.

1. Make the following points about each passage in this section:
- Daniel 10:11–13, 20—The "prince of the Persian kingdom" is apparently one of the evil angels.
- John 12:31—Satan is called the "prince of this world."
- Matthew 4:8–10—Jesus did not dispute Satan's claim to possess worldly kingdoms. Remind the participants that, even though Satan exercises much power in this sinful world, and even though hell is spoken of as his kingdom as well, Satan does not reign supreme. God has dominion over all things—even hell.

2. Explore together the verses that follow the question "How does Satan try to lure us into his kingdom?"
- John 8:42–44—Satan is the father of lies.
- 1 John 4:3—Satan does not acknowledge that Jesus is Lord.
- Genesis 3:1–5—Satan tempts us to be like God; he appeals to our pride.

3. Ephesians 6 describes the "full armor of God"—truth, righteousness, readiness, faith, salvation, the Word of God, and prayer. This armor is given by the Holy Spirit to those who believe in Jesus Christ and will help us defend ourselves in the fight against evil angels. As participants share what they found, answers will be varied and personal. Invite volunteers to share but do not require anyone to do so. Also ask, "Which of these weapons do you think is your most effective resource? Why?"

The Angel of the LORD

Distribute copies of Resource Page 4B and direct the group's attention to the first paragraph. Have a volunteer read it aloud, or do so yourself. Then assign each passage to an individual, pair, or small group. Challenge them to identify the clues in the passage that "the angel of the LORD" is really God Himself. After allowing time for their study, let the participants report on their passages. The clues they will likely identify are as follows:
- Genesis 16:7–11—God speaks in the first person to promise Hagar countless descendants (verse 10).
- Genesis 22:11–12—God stops Abraham from sacrificing Isaac, noting that he did not withhold "from Me your only son." Abraham's "sacrifice" of Isaac was not to any angel, but to God.
- Genesis 31:11–13—The "angel" says plainly, "I am the God of Bethel"—that is, the God Jacob's father worshiped at Bethel.
- Exodus 3:1–6—The angel in verse 2 reveals Himself as God in verse 4 and following verses.
- Numbers 22:20–35 (especially verses 20 and 35)—In verses 20 and 35, the words of God and those of the angel of the LORD are nearly identical—"Do [say] only what I tell you."

- Judges 6:11–16—In this conversation with Gideon, the identity of the angel is gradually revealed to be God Himself.
- Zechariah 3:1–4—In verse 4, the "angel" tells Zechariah that He has "taken away" Joshua's sins, something only God can do.

Emphasize to the participants that whether He speaks or acts directly or through angels, God is still the one at work in every instance. Our concern is to not gain an inaccurate picture of angels from these Old Testament manifestations of God.

God's Final Victory

Direct the participants to Revelation 4–5. Point out the craft materials or art supplies you have assembled. Invite them—in pairs, small groups, or individually, as you choose—to use the materials to recreate this heavenly scene. Remind them that they will have only about 10 minutes for their work. (If craft and art supplies are not available, or if your participants need a "running start," distribute copies of Resource Page 4C. Invite the participants to add to this "starter picture" whatever details they wish from Revelation 4–5, using a pencil or pen.)

In an intergenerational group, invite participants from the same family—or from two of three families—to team up to recreate the scene.

After their work is substantially completed, invite the participants to display their work for the rest of the group. Read, or have a volunteer read, these two short, powerful chapters of John's vision as the participants admire each other's efforts. After the reading, remind the group of these three important points:

- In John's vision we see the angels of God in their most "natural" work—praising God Almighty and Jesus, the Lamb, who was slain for our sins and the sins of all people.
- Later in John's vision, the angels are described as assisting God as at least four "versions" of the history of the church unfold.
- The final result in each version is the same—Satan is vanquished and Jesus reigns supreme over a new heaven and a new earth. Truly He is worthy of the praise of countless angels and all the saints—us and all those who have gone before and will come after.

Closing Worship

Close with the following prayer: "Dear Jesus, help us to study Your Word so that we may know the truth and not be deceived by evil angels. Move us to pray for strength to fight against evil and keep us in Your Word as our source of strength. Remind us of the promise of Your Word, 'The One who is in you is greater than the one who is in the world.' We praise You for Your victory on the cross over Satan and all evil. We thank You for our lives of faith here on earth, and the life eternal we will enjoy with You in heaven. Help us to be faithful servants. We ask it in Your name, Jesus. Amen."

You may also wish to sing the hymn "Stand Up, Stand Up for Jesus."

Extending the Lesson

There are a number of books available with angel stories that affirm the truths taught in the Bible:

The Hiding Place, by Corrie ten Boom

Angels, by Billy Graham

What the Bible Says about Angels, by David Jeremiah

Angels among Us, by Ron Rhodes

When Angels Appear, by Hope MacDonald

Locate two or three such stories and share them with the class. Invite them to use the knowledge they have gained from this study course to identify the ways in which angels are being used by God in each story. In what ways is the faith of the people involved strengthened? (Not everything in every book, however, depicts angels accurately. Choose your material carefully.)

Satan's Kingdom

Evil angels are real! They are not naughty angels that are cute or funny, but evil forces to fight against. Angels are sometimes called the "heavenly host," a well-organized *army*. Why would God need an army if there were nothing to fight against? Satan's powers are limited to this world, but they are very real.

1. What do these passages say about Satan's kingdom?

- Daniel 10:11–13, 20

- John 12:31

- Matthew 4:8–10

2. How might Satan try to lure us into his kingdom?

- John 8:42–44

- 1 John 4:3

- Genesis 3:1–5

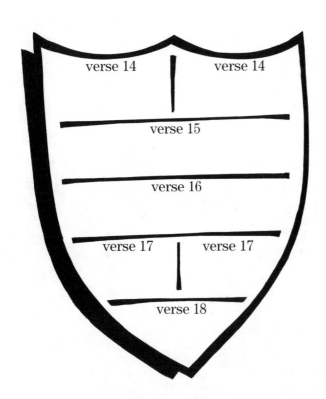

verse 14   verse 14

verse 15

verse 16

verse 17   verse 17

verse 18

3. Study Ephesians 6:12–17 to find out what weapons we have in the fight against evil angels. List each of these weapons in a different section of the shield. Be prepared to suggest a practical way that each spiritual tool could be better employed in your life.

The Angel of the LORD

In the Old Testament there are frequent references to "the angel of the LORD." Many of these passages clearly describe the One who is over all things including angels. When the angel of the LORD speaks as God Himself in the first person, doing or saying things only God Himself can do or say, it is clearly a manifestation of God Himself, not one of His heavenly creatures.

In the following Bible passages, discover the clues that indicate that the "angel" might be God Himself.

- Genesis 16:7–11

- Genesis 22:11–12

- Genesis 31:11–13

- Exodus 3:1–6

- Numbers 22:20–35 (especially verses 20 and 35)

- Judges 6:11–16

- Zechariah 3:1–4

As we study the Bible and learn about angels, we do well not to confuse these references to God with the passages that describe angels and their work.

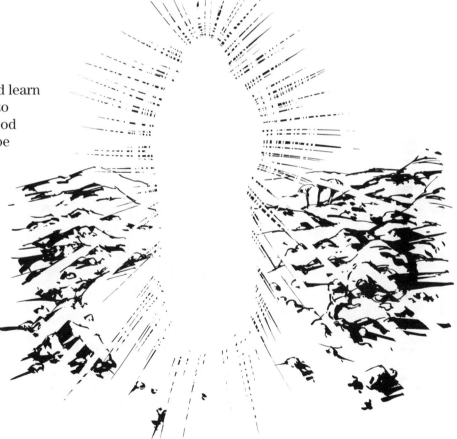

All about **Angels**

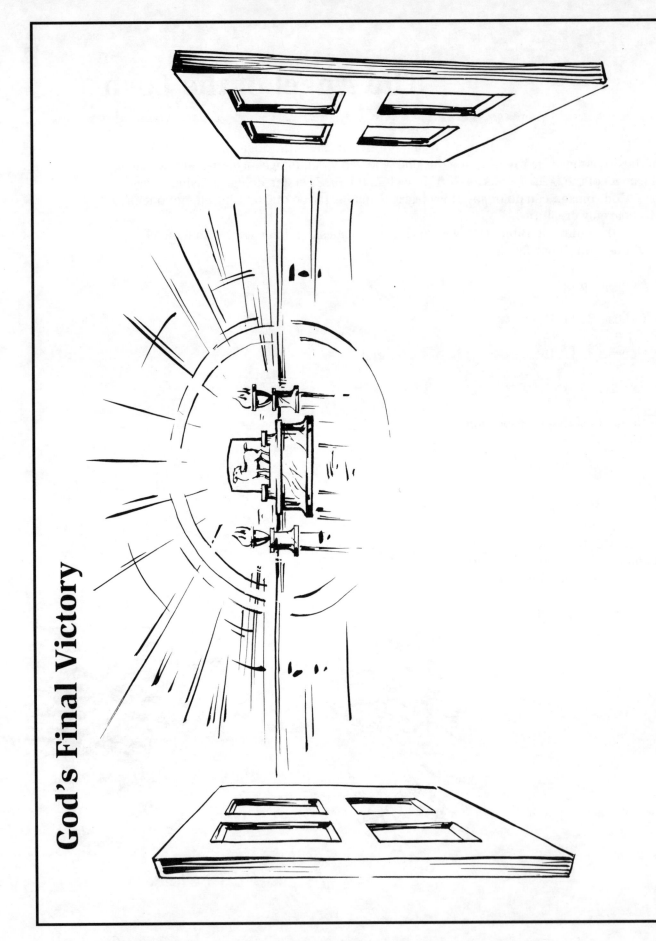

God's Final Victory